ideals®
VALENTINE

There's something that lives in a valentine,
A heartwarming message sincere,
When it's sent to a special friend or friends,
On Valentine's Day of the year.

Each traditional word, thought, and meaning,
Passed along through channels of time,
Have become quite a social acceptance,
We question no reason or rhyme.

But the motive expressed in the custom,
As it was in the days of old,
Gives a valentine such a high rating,
That it carries its weight in gold.

And the fancy red heart made of paper,
Trimmed with ever delicate lace,
Containing a short sentimental note,
Finds its chosen person and place.

Yet the price that is paid is no factor,
If the sender can but convey
Exactly the way he feels from within,
Through greetings on Valentine's Day.

Anton J. Stoffle

Editorial Director, James Kuse

Managing Editor, Ralph Luedtke

Editor/Ideals, Colleen Callahan Gonring

Associate Editor, Linda Robinson

Production Editor/Manager, Richard Lawson

Photographic Editor, Gerald Koser

Copy Editor, Norma Barnes

Art Editor, Duane Weaver

ISBN 0-89542-329-4 295

IDEALS—Vol. 37 No. 1 January MCMLXXX, IDEALS (ISSN 0019-137X) is published eight times a year,
January, February, April, June, July, September, October, November
by IDEALS PUBLISHING CORPORATION, 11315 Watertown Plank Road, Milwaukee, Wis. 53226
Second class postage paid at Milwaukee, Wisconsin. Copyright © MCMLXXIX by IDEALS PUBLISHING CORPORATION.
Postmaster, please send form 3579 to Ideals Publishing Corporation, 175 Community Drive, Great Neck, New York, 11025
All rights reserved. Title IDEALS registered U.S. Patent Office.
Published simultaneously in Canada.

ONE YEAR SUBSCRIPTION—eight consecutive issues as published—only $15.95
TWO YEAR SUBSCRIPTION—sixteen consecutive issues as published—only $27.95
SINGLE ISSUES—only $2.95

Daily Valentines

Once a year we turn our thoughts
To a valentine,
A dainty card of lace and verse
Where dreams and love entwine.
'Tis like a lovely sweet refrain
Singing in each heart;
We choose our valentine with care
To play its special part.
Sometimes it's made with little hands and,
Oh, the effort there!
Though full of paste and crooked print,
It's beautiful and fair.
Sometimes it may be purchased
And selected carefully
To send upon its merry way
For our loved ones to see.
Each valentine has magic
And contains three priceless things . . .
Love and joy and memories
That caring always brings.

LaVerne P. Larson

A Valentine

How sweet to get a valentine
Of plain or fancy art,
A rose so pink and violets, too,
Or satin-covered heart.

But more than beauty or design,
We prize the words that say
The sender's love comes with the gift
In quite the warmest way.

We like to know that someone cares,
That someone wants to do
The kindly deed that makes us feel
Well loved and happy, too.

So why not give expression then,
To love for friends so dear,
Not only on one certain day
But many times a year?

Our valentines may be a smile,
A cheerful word or two,
A helping hand, a tender glance
That signals, "I love you."

And if we often take the time
To give these friendly signs,
The world will soon be brightened by
Our daily valentines.

Cleo King

Ruth Blandin Field

A name associated with Ideals for many years, Ruth Blandin Field was born in Gorham, New Hampshire in 1899. She attended local schools and taught for ten years in Maine and New Hampshire, later becoming principal of Tilden Elementary School in Keene, New Hampshire. She married Winfred Field in 1927 and reared three children. Ruth Field began writing poetry at the age of nine, and has had her poems published in many New England periodicals. An Ideals contributor for over thirty years, Mrs. Field has delighted readers with her honest, heartwarming verses, usually extolling old-fashioned, traditional values. When one of her poems, "The Queen's Pocketbook," found its way into the hands of Queen Elizabeth of England, she received a response from Buckingham Palace expressing how much the Queen enjoyed the poem. Mrs. Field was surprised to find "royal grandchildren much like my own." Still energetic and involved, Ruth Field is active in many literary and educational associations as well as doing volunteer work for senior citizens in her community. A teacher, mother, grandmother, and poet, Mrs. Field remains an inspiration to all who read and enjoy her poetry.

Tenderly

The heart is a storehouse brimful of treasure,
Deep understanding and warm flow of love,
Long ago filled with unstinted measure,
Its courage and patience a gift from above.
Always, oh always, remember that giving
Of the heart's treasure can make life worthwhile,
Each is endowed with the sweet joy of living,
Hurts can be mended with a bright smile.
Over deep silence, across darkest gloom,
Hearts speak a language, tender and good,
For each is a chalice, God's secret room,
And sends forth a message by all understood.
Tenderly, then, let the heart speak,
Say what it will, love will hold sway,
Forceful the word of the kindly and meek
For tender hearts know and show man the way.

Who Walks With Love

Who walks with love
Knows peace and joy,
Finds much of worth in simple things;
Possesses faith with no alloy,
And in the heart life's glory sings.
Deep understanding goes with love,
Gives insight into friend or foe,
Adds courage to surmount all ills.
On rugged ways where we must go,
There is some beauty everywhere
For loving hearts, below, above,
A psalmody with all to share
For him who walks with love.

Hearts, Old and New

From a hidden, dusty nook
Beneath the mellowed eaves
I found a quaint, old-fashioned book
And, pressed between its leaves,
A valentine of long ago
That showed an old-time art
With paper lace and azure bow,
A lavish crimson heart,
With golden arrow, cupid, too,
An old-time maid and man,
Forget-me-nots and feverfew,
And, inside, words that ran:
"Oh, fairest damsel, here's my heart,
Yours to keep, you are divine,
Tell me that we'll never part,
Will you be my valentine?"
Wisps of lace, a satin bow
On our valentines today,
Cupids, flowers, golden darts
Still the same old story say.
Let times change us as they will,
Folks adopt a modern line,
But maidens still all feel the thrill
At "Will you be my valentine?"

Messages of Love

Upon this very special day
The wintry winds may blow,
But cannot chill the happy thrill
In hearts that are aglow
Because of messages that shine
Where flowers brightly twine,
Midst lace and hearts
And Cupid's darts
Upon a valentine.
The old, old messages of love
That always thrill anew,
That right all wrong,
Fill life with song,
The magic of I love you.

As In a Crystal Jar

Like rose leaves in a scented crystal jar,
The heart will keep its cherished memories,
And though loved ones must sometimes go afar,
The heart still keeps life's sweetest melodies.
The song of love played on sweet springtime's lute,
With beauty everlasting seems to sing;
Its cadence whispering notes on magic flute
Which time would banish past remembering.
The mind too often dims through passing years,
And, like pale mists, the interim between
The first and last, its blended joy and tears,
Life's fragments lie, forgotten and unseen.
But in the heart that truly loved still gleams
The fragrant petals of our faded dreams,
For all lovers, young and old,
As in a crystal jar to sweetly hold.

The Red, Red Rose

Oh red, red rose upon the stem,
Oh queen among the flowers . . .
Will you bless my love with happiness
And beautify her hours?

Oh fragrant bloom of love and youth,
Oh beauty so divine . . .
Will you bring gladness to her heart
With a tingling joy sublime?

Oh deep within your rosy blush
That glorifies the stem,
Will you convey a thought of love
I cannot phrase with voice or pen?

Oh red, red rose of queenly grace
That glows beneath the sky above,
Within your own majestic way,
Will you whisper of my love?

Joy Belle Burgess

Floral Symbols of Love
Legends and Lore

Daisy

The daisy is on the whole the favorite flower of all British poets. Spenser, for one, speaks kindly of "the little daizie that at evening closes."

A well-known practice of maids who have lost their hearts, wishing to determine whether they are ever to receive recompense, is to pluck one by one the petals from the daisy, chanting, "He loves me—loves me not," the while. The last petal and the last phrase determine the situation.

The daisy is the flower of the "Maid Marguerite, meek and mild" of Antioch, whose prayers for women about to become mothers saved many lives and enshrined her in their love.

Spring has not arrived until you can set your foot on twelve daisies.

To dream of daisies in springtime or summer is a lucky omen; but to dream of them in fall or winter portends ill.

In Thuringia, upon the extraction of a tooth, a person must eat three daisies to be henceforth free from toothache.

King Henry the Eighth consumed many daisies in a futile effort to rid himself of ulcers.

Violet

The violet, as a symbol of faithfulness, has been celebrated by no less a poet than Shakespeare himself:

> Violet is for Faithfulness,
> Which in me shall abide;
> Hoping, likewise, that from your heart
> You will not let it slide.

Some lovely maids of antiquity once became the objects of Venus' queenly wrath, when a dispute arose whether she or they were the more beautiful. Cupid judged in favor of the maidens; and in a fury, Venus beat them until they were blue. Thus the girls became the first violets; this, anyway, is the story as Herrick tells it.

The most glorious of the Greeks regarded the violet with extreme favor, and preferred for themselves above all other names that of "Athenian crowned with Violets."

A garland of violets, worn about the head, prevents dizziness.

Where roses and violets bloom in autumn, an epidemic will follow within the year.

Bullein's advice concerning violets is as follows: "Take of the water of violet flowers, of fine sugar sodden and clarified, mingle them, and seethe therein with a soft fire. This is a pleasant remedy in all burning Agues."

Rose

The origin of the red rose has been variously explained. The ancients believed it to have been stained by Venus' blood, when her fingers were wounded by its thorns. Herrick gives a more cheerful explanation:

> As Cupid danced among
> The Gods, he down the nectar flung;
> Which on the white rose being shed,
> Made it, forever after, red.

The rose is a symbol of fidelity, as well as an expression of beauty: it is said that the roses of Virginia will die if transplanted.

King Edward the Sixth's perfume is made thusly: Take 12 spoonfuls of bright red rosewater, the weight of sixpence in fine powder sugar, and boil it on hot embers and coals softly, and the room will smell as though it were full of roses. But you must burn a sweet cypress wood before, to take away the gross air.

A love potion, made of red and white rose leaves and forget-me-nots, boiled in 385 drops of water for the sixteenth part of an hour, will, if properly made, insure the love of one of the opposite sex, if three drops of the mixture are put into something the person is to drink.

Forget-Me-Not

The meaning of the forget-me-not is easily seen from its name; and there is a story explaining how the name came to be. A young man and his maid walked one day along the Danube, when the girl spied some lovely flowers on the opposite bank and made known her desire for them. The youth swam the stream, picked a bunch of the precious blossoms, and struck out again across the raging river. A huge wave bore down upon him and carried him off toward the Black Sea. It was all he could do to fling the bouquet at the feet of his beloved, crying, "Forget me not!" as he disappeared from view. The maiden made a chain of the flowers which she wore always; and she never forgot him, if legend can be believed.

If one takes a sojourn in Egypt near the 27th day of their month Thoth (which is near to our month of August), and he anoints his eyes with the flower forget-me-not, he will be made to see visions. At least so it was in ancient times.

It is thought among the Germans, who lack perhaps the element of romance in their floral legends, that the name "forget-me-not" derives from the nauseous taste which that flower leaves in the mouth. Yet these same Germans are apt to plant the forget-me-not on their graves, so as to be remembered; which seems to indicate some caprice or else irony of spirit.

A. Stoddard Kull

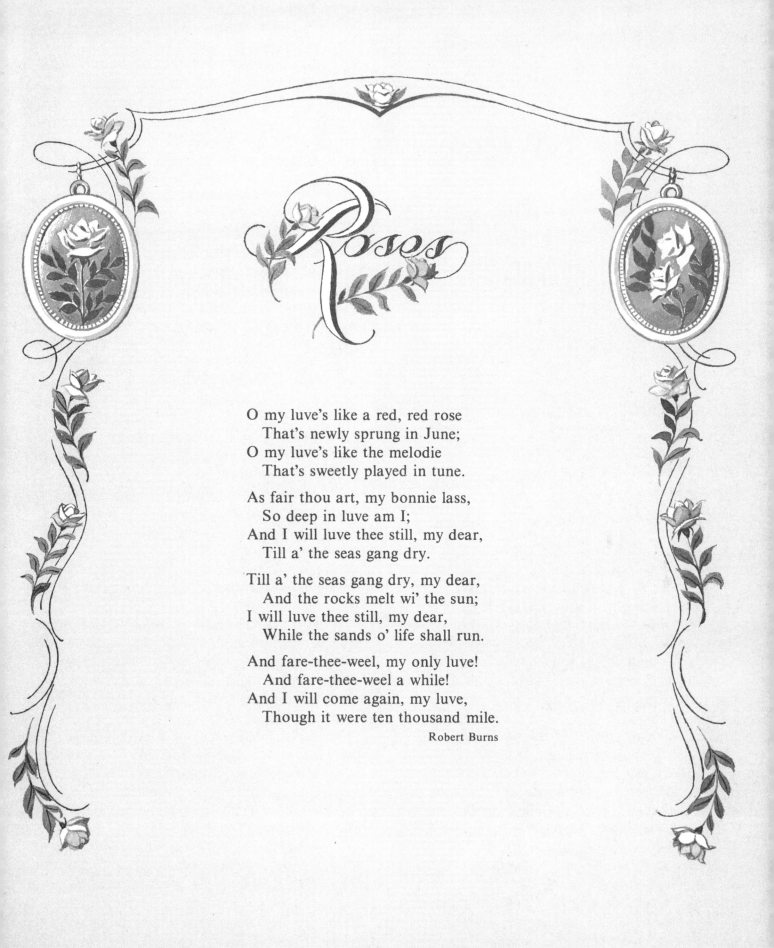

Roses

O my luve's like a red, red rose
   That's newly sprung in June;
O my luve's like the melodie
   That's sweetly played in tune.

As fair thou art, my bonnie lass,
   So deep in luve am I;
And I will luve thee still, my dear,
   Till a' the seas gang dry.

Till a' the seas gang dry, my dear,
   And the rocks melt wi' the sun;
I will luve thee still, my dear,
   While the sands o' life shall run.

And fare-thee-weel, my only luve!
   And fare-thee-weel a while!
And I will come again, my luve,
   Though it were ten thousand mile.

Robert Burns

SNIP, SNIP...
SCHERENSCHNITTE

R. A. Baumgart

Where have all the scherenschnitters gone? The old scissors cutting artists just aren't around anymore. Maybe it's the affluence, maybe it's a lack of patience brought about by the hurried pace of modern living, maybe too many potential artisans have reverted to viewing rather than doing. It's certainly not a lack of appreciation for the ancient folk art form of giving expression to creative ideas by snipping colorful or intricate designs out of paper.

Folk art speaks for itself. It doesn't need words to describe the color and form. Color and form tell a story, the story of common people creating from their hearts and from their minds.

Scissors cutting had been practiced in much of Europe for centuries. It reached a peak of popularity about 200 years ago. It belonged to the people. The Poles called it wycinanki; the Germans and Swiss called it scherenschnitte.

Polish peasants longed for creative fulfillment. They reached out for color and beauty to brighten their lives. Polish peasant women bartered spare vegetables or an extra chicken or goose from their small farms for highly prized colored paper. The colored paper could be exchanged with that saved by other peasants until the desired shades had been collected.

During the long winter nights when wind and snow ruled the Polish countryside, when cold squeezed through every crack and crevice of crowded huts, by dim lamplight or flickering candle, wycinanki was born. Subjects tended to emulate beauty and color from the peasants' daily lives. Birds, flowers or geometric patterns were popular. Earthy shades of sky blue, grass green, reds and yellows for flowers and birds were most preferred.

The "folded" technique was common. A single sheet of colored paper was usually trimmed to a circle, It was then folded into multiple layers. Patterns were carefully sketched on the exposed surface of the top layer. Calloused hands, accustomed to gripping the hoe, the rake or the shovel, now carefully guided the scissors along pattern lines and snipped out the design.

The process was repeated with other colored papers and other patterns. When all the pieces had been carefully cut they were assembled in proper order and painstakingly glued together to form the completed wycinanki piece.

Wycinanki tells the story of Polish peasants living in crowded huts with whitewashed walls and tiny windows. Wycinanki were often used to frame doors and windows. The pieces could easily be changed with the seasons and replaced with new wycinanki to commemorate special events or religious observances.

Among the Gemans and Swiss, scissor cutting, or scherenschnitte, tended to be more delicate and more detailed in design. Scherenschnitte was cut from single sheets of paper and pasted on a contrasting paper background. Common subjects were fantasies of trees, elves or rural scenes.

Pattern outlines were first drawn on paper, then snipped out with the scissors. Many of the works were symmetrical, or balanced. This effect was achieved by folding the paper to be cut and snipping out the pattern on both parts of the paper simultaneously.

Some dedicated artists departed from the traditional. They rejected the folded technique and insisted upon cutting only a single unfolded sheet. These finished pieces can be incredibly detailed. Each tiny leaf, each minute twig of each tree is traced and cut out as one finished piece. The finished asymmetrical work resulted in a more natural, realistic design.

Most of these old works were snipped from white paper and attached to a black background. Some artists reversed the color combinations by preferring to cut from black paper and attach the design to a white background. Others used a variety of combinations such as a black design on a gold background, black design on a pastel pink background, a white design on a blue background or a white design on a burnt orange background.

Scissor cutting periodically experienced a mild surge of popularity. Wycinanki creations have been marketed through the Polish Art Bureau and have become rather popular with tourists. Wycinanki has been found in Polish neighborhoods where it had been imported and sold at fairs or fund raising projects.

A few of the early scherenschnitte pieces are exhibited in European museums. Most have been hidden from public view carefully tucked away as heirlooms in nearly forgotten trunks in secluded attics.

Scherenschnitte is a demanding art form. The work is incredibly detailed. Long hours and exacting conditions are required. Fine detail demands that cutting be done by natural light. An average size cutting may require upward of one million well directed snips of the tiny scissors. Patience isn't a virtue—it is a necessity. One tiny slip of the scissors and a whole piece can be ruined. The hand that guides the scissors must be the envy of any surgeon.

The ultimate in scherenschnitte is collage. Few artists even attempted it. As a result collages have become exceedingly rare, and are a highly prized collector's item.

Collage is the combination of variously colored papers cut into the component parts making up one finished multicolored piece. Up to 100 different colored papers could be used in preparing one of the collage masterpieces.

The true artists resisted the tempting shortcut of merely painting the different shadings of color on the various parts of a flowered collage. The preparation of a collage is highly complex. Thousands of separate pieces must be cut from the various colored papers. They must then be carefully assembled, fitted and mounted on the background paper.

Some of the old European masters preferred to use designs requiring only a few colors of paper to minimize complexity in mounting. Others resorted

to painting desired shadings of color in the design with watercolors. Comparison of scherenschnitte is difficult because so few examples of this unique art form are to be found in galleries of Europe or in the United States.

A generation ago American school children traditionally practiced a basic form of scissor cutting by cutting out lacey valentines. Even this once-a-year event tends to use less and less of the homemade product as technology now supplies a prodigious quantity of mass-produced valentines at reasonable prices.

More and more homes are being brightened with a greater variety of oils, watercolors and sculpture. The increased interest in art offers new hope for the vanishing tradition of scissor cutting.

Wycinanki, imported from Poland, has generated interest in the old Polish folk art form. It has even induced some Americans to revive scissor cutting locally.

Scherenschnitte pieces exhibited at art shows find eager buyers. If the trend continues, the good hausfrau might again notice that her little sewing scissors have a habit of disappearing. She might find them in eager young hands trying to revive a lost tradition.

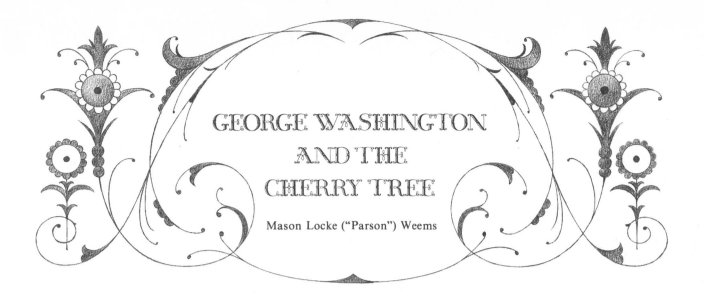

GEORGE WASHINGTON AND THE CHERRY TREE

Mason Locke ("Parson") Weems

The following anecdote is a case in point. It is too valuable to be lost, and too true to be doubted, for it was communicated to me by the same excellent lady to whom I am indebted for the last.

"When George," said she, "was about six years old, he was made the wealthy master of a hatchet of which, like most little boys, he was immoderately fond, and was constantly going about chopping everything that came in his way. One day, in the garden, where he often amused himself hacking his mother's pea-sticks, he unluckily tried the edge of his hatchet on the body of a beautiful young English cherry tree, which he barked so terribly, that I don't believe the tree ever got the better of it. The next morning the old gentleman, finding out what had befallen his tree, which, by the by, was a great favorite, came into the house and with much warmth asked for the mischievous author, declaring at the same time that he would not have taken five guineas for his tree. Nobody could tell him anything about it. Presently George and his hatchet made their appearance. 'George,' said his father, 'do you know who killed that beautiful little cherry tree yonder in the garden?' This was a tough question; and George staggered under it for a moment, but quickly recovered himself; and looking at his father, with the sweet face of youth brightened with the inexpressible charm of all-conquering truth, he bravely cried out, 'I can't tell a lie, Pa. You know I can't tell a lie. I did cut it with my hatchet.'—'Run to my arms, you dearest boy,' cried his father in transports, 'run to my arms; glad am I, George, that you killed my tree; for you have paid me for it a thousand fold. Such an act of heroism in my son is more worth than a thousand trees, though blossomed with silver, and their fruits of purest gold.' "

From The Life of George Washington

Cherry Pie

Line a 9-inch pie pan with pastry and brush with egg white. Set aside. Measure 6 c. frozen unsweetened pie cherries and let thaw. Mix together cornstarch, salt, brown sugar, almond flavoring, and butter. Add cherries and bring to a boil, stirring carefully. Pour while boiling into prepared crust. To decorate pie with hatchets as in photo, roll out remaining dough and cut with a cookie cutter. Bake at 425° for about 25 minutes, or until edge is brown.

Pastry for a two-crust 9-inch pie
6 c. frozen unsweetened pie cherries
2½ T. cornstarch
⅛ t. salt
1 c. brown sugar
¼ t. almond flavoring
1 T. butter

Snow Ice Cream

You may talk about the beauty
Of the snowy countryside;
Laugh at the crooked snowmen
Made wherever children bide.

But the beauty and the laughter
Are but a single part
Of the reason that a snowfall
Thrills my aging heart.

For the glowing, golden memory
That thrills me now, as then,
Is the cold, sweet-tasting goodness
Mother made again and again.

From the most protected banks
Unsullied by soot or tracks,
She scooped the snow up gently,
Not letting the soft stuff pack;

A few drops of vanilla, some
Sugar, milk or cream,
And we children all got ready
For the winter taste supreme.

Flat on our little stomachs
Before the blazing fire,
We savored delicious snow ice cream
To our childish hearts' desire.

Yes, I love the sparkling beauty,
The snow scene soft and white;
But I would really give a fortune
For Mother's snow ice cream tonight!

Marion G. White

Valentine's Day

This is a special day of love
When heart calls out to heart,
A day when saucy Cupid aims
A sugar-sweetened dart.

This is a day when flowering plums
Perfume deep memories,
When honeyed words most coyly slip
From tongues that Cupid frees.

When young and old banquet on love,
Served in a crystal dream,
When Cupid teases with his bow,
And whips life's hidden cream.

Josepha Murray Emms

Heart-shaped Sponge Cake

1 c. warm water
2 c. flour
3 t. baking powder
½ t. salt
6 eggs, separated
½ t. cream of tartar
2 c. sugar
1 t. vanilla

Sift together flour, baking powder and salt. Beat egg whites with cream of tartar. Add ½ cup of the sugar. Set aside. Beat egg yolks until blended. Add sugar and vanilla. Beat 4 to 5 minutes. Add dry ingredients, egg whites and warm water. Bake in a greased and floured heart-shaped tube pan. Bake in a 350° oven for 60 to 70 minutes.

Boiled Icing

½ c. sugar
2 egg whites
2 T. water
1 7-oz. jar marshmallow creme
½ t. vanilla

Combine sugar, egg whites and water in top of a double boiler. Beat with electric mixer over boiling water until soft peaks form. Add marshmallow creme and beat to stiff peaks. Remove from heat. Beat in vanilla.

In the Beginning . . .

Catherine Otten

". . . and they lived happily ever after!" For fifty-eight busy, struggling, joyful, exciting, fearful, impulsive, emotional years, they lived happily together!

A goat had brought these two lovers together just before the turn of the century. Frank, a tall, handsome, young lad was obliged to take Matti, the family goat, to an empty lot for grazing each morning, and fetch her home each evening. Helen, a pretty slip of a girl, watched him each day as he and his goat passed her home. It wasn't long before Frank began noticing this attractive little miss, and soon their shy greetings turned into longer and longer vists over the fence.

One day, Helen was busy sweeping the walk near the fence, eagerly waiting for Frank's evening stop, when Matti came trotting down the road dragging her torn rope behind her. She headed straight for the fence and Helen compliantly tied the rope to a picket just as the breathless, long-legged Frank arrived.

"Thank you," he cried. "I tied her to the hitching post while I went into the butcher shop," he explained. "Matti must have been as impatient to get here as I was," he added as he examined the frayed end of the rope. "I can't say I blame her, Helen. She likes you, and so do I."

"I'm so glad," Helen replied, blushing prettily as she handed Frank a glass of cool water. "I was hoping you would come to our church picnic Sunday. Could you? Mama said I could ask you."

More picnics followed. Long walks in the park, band concerts, ice cream socials, dances, and hay rides kept these two lovers together. As their friendship grew, they discovered their many mutual likes and dislikes.

Those were the days that parents selected mates for their children. However, Helen and Frank asserted their independence one day by announcing that they would marry each other and no one else. Helen's parents knew it was useless to try to change her mind. Frank's parents, after numerous discussions, decided to go along with their decision, too.

Helen told her children many times about their wedding day. "The day was beautiful—cool, fresh and full of sunshine. I was so thrilled as I watched Frank coming across the yard to get me. We went to St. Vincent's Church on Mitchell Street in a very grand hack drawn by two spirited horses. It was the first day of May in 1900. Our wedding was very simple. A few of our relatives and friends listened to us repeat our vows.

"For better, for worse, for richer, for poorer, until death do us part—" we solemnly promised from the bottom of our full, happy hearts.

"We returned to my home in the same pretty hack. My father who had hurried away before we left the church, met us at the door with a loaf of bread and a dish of salt.

"Bless you, my children" he said as he handed us these gifts.

"This offering is guaranteed to keep the wolf away from your door. May it always be true."

"Frank's father then came and stood next to him. Our two fathers extended their hands over us, and gave us their parental blessings as we entered the house.

"The wedding celebration began with a hearty breakfast, and continued throughout the day. Early in the evening, there was a sudden and deafening clattering noise in the yard.

"It's a shivaree," screamed the children as they ran out on the porch. There were pots and pans and tin cans being banged together. Dinner bells and cowbells rang. Wooden spoons were banging on pails and dishpans.

"The bride and groom—we want to see the bride and groom," the crowd shouted. "Come out!" The noise became louder and the crowd became more boisterous.

"The minute we stepped out on the porch, we were showered with rice and more noise. There were grown-ups and children, all banging on something. My new brother-in-law, our best man, came out with handsful of pennies and threw them out at the crowd. The ladies who were helping cook the wedding meals also came to the rescue and satisfied the noisemakers with plates of cookies. The noise outside continued long after we went back into the house to get on with the celebration. Dancing, eating and drinking continued all night. The guests never left until the sun began to light up the morning sky.

"It was a wonderful wedding," Mama would finish dreamily.

Love's Old Sweet Song

Once in the dear dead days beyond recall,
　When on the world the mists began to fall,
Out of the dreams that rose in happy throng,
　Low to our hearts Love sang an old sweet song;
And in the dusk where fell the firelight gleam,
　Softly it wove itself into our dream.

Chorus:
Just a song at twilight, when the lights are low,
　And the flick'ring shadows softly come and go,
Tho' the heart be weary, sad the day and long,
　Still to us at twilight comes Love's old song,
　　Comes Love's old sweet song.

Even today we hear Love's song of yore,
　Deep in our hearts it dwells for evermore,
Footsteps may falter, weary grows the way,
　Still we can hear it at the close of day;
Still to the end when life's dim shadows fall,
　Love will be found the sweetest song of all.

Chorus:
Just a song at twilight, when the lights are low,
　And the flick'ring shadows softly come and go,
Tho' the heart be weary, sad the day and long,
　Still to us at twilight comes Love's old song,
　　Comes Love's old sweet song.

J. Clifton Bingham

Love and Courtship in America

The Valentine

Valentine's Day, named for a saint and sacred to lovers, was once celebrated by a young man asking the first lady he encountered in the morning—and he made sure to meet a certain lady—to be his valentine; if she consented he acted as her escort throughout the day, bought her sweetmeats, and entertained her attentively. As an offshoot of this custom decorated letters and poems were sent to ask a lady (or a gentleman) to be one's valentine.

At first these were always of one's own devising. Then the stationers provided embossed, paper-lace-edged sheets to write them on. They took the form of hearts. They bore emblems of doves, cupids, and flowers. Finally, about a century and a half ago, stock valentines were printed to save the lazy swain the trouble of making them. There were even comic valentines to send in fun or malice. Guessing the sender was not always too difficult!

The Parlor Sofa

Even in the face of the record it seems hardly possible that this piece of furniture played so important a part in bringing young people together! Its horsehair covering—to judge from examples which survive—was ill adapted to hold a sitter more than a minute before he began to slide. Its rosewood curves bore no correspondence whatsoever to those of the human body. Yet almost every young couple between 1855 and 1880 spent many a dreamy session on one, further hampered by hoopskirts, bustles, and tight military uniforms.

The sofa was presumed to allow seclusion, standing as it did in a room generally cold, stuffy, and shut up. Lucky were the lovers who were left alone there. Young brothers crept in and had to be bribed to leave. Mother might find it good for a change to come into the parlor to knit, father to read. Like as not, when a young man visited, the parlor became a center of family activity. Even if it were to the family's advantage to have "the question popped," curiosity drew it in.

The Buggy Ride

With the incidence of the buggy ride we come almost to the horseless carriage and the modern era, its customs of courtship so much at variance with those of the past. The buggy ride had manifest dangers for a young woman, no less real than those of a ride in a horseless carriage. In the first place, chaperones could not go along because it was understood that there was no room for them. Then the vehicle might meet with an accident. The horse might run away or lose a shoe so that one could be stranded on a lonely country road. Buggy rides were not only hazardous, they were very popular.

A young man who could get possession of a horse and buggy—not every family owned one; they were something of a luxury—knew that he had gone a good way toward making his reputation as a gay Lothario. From such a young man, bold, enterprising, a driver of mettled horseflesh, what might not be expected? It was a high-spirited, self-reliant young woman who mustered courage to go out with him.

The Language of Flowers

Hill's Manual states, "A very charming and interesting method of communicating thought is by the aid of flowers, their language and sentiment being understood by the parties who present them." Yet it may be doubted whether a courtship was ever so carried to completion, for the vocabulary was necessarily limited to blossoms in season; a lover searching for just the right word might have had to delay a year to say it with flowers.

There were of course certain common garden favorites generally available: forget-me-not with a message in its name, roses with a variety of tender meaning (save the yellow, which signified waning love), and ivy, always on hand even in dead of winter, expressing a desire for matrimony. But would it not have been a rare lover who had patience for this sort of thing? Certainly the messages in the pages of a floral dictionary were not to be preferred to those spoken in a soft voice in the arms of one's beloved! The bouquet of significance was merely a lover's fragrant aid.

Paul McPharlin

Valentine Memories

Garnett Ann Schultz

What have you saved in memories
Throughout the passing years,
Perhaps a moment rich in love
Or one of hurts and fears;
The precious thoughts that linger,
Of laughter sweet and true,
A lasting dream from yesterday
That meant so much to you?

What have you tucked away, dear one,
Within that loving heart,
A lock of hair, a picture rare,
Life's very richest part,
A vision still to cherish,
One sweet enchanting look,
Perhaps a rose you gently pressed
In pages of a book?

For memories do linger
As years would come and go,
The pleasant ones that live and last
Because we need them so.
Life ever holds true meaning,
Tomorrows sweet and yet,
It's lovely treasured memories
We never quite forget.

Elizabeth Barrett & Robert Browning

Some unlucky persons die with a great treasure of love and devotion unspent. Except for a miracle, this would have happened to both Elizabeth Barrett and Robert Browning. Each was passionate and eloquent; each nearly missed finding the beloved person on whom to spend these riches. Had they not met and married—far along in life to be marrying for the first time—it is almost certain that neither one would ever have loved or married anyone.

They were made for one another. They were equally much in love and equally articulate in giving expression to their mutual adoration. They are the only great lovers who wrote their own love story. It is there for us to read in their letters and their poems, especially in Mrs. Browning's "Sonnets from the Portuguese." Surely these ardent and moving verses are the most wonderful present any woman ever gave to her lover. Yet they were given in return for his even more wonderful gift to her: life itself.

An invalid and a recluse when she and Browning met, Elizabeth thought that Death would be her only bridegroom. In the first Sonnet she wrote:

. . . a voice said in mastery, while I strove,
"Guess now who holds thee?" "Death," I said.
But, there the silver answer rang,
"Not Death, but Love."

Elizabeth Barrett was born six years before Robert Browning, in 1806. Her mother was a vague, indistinct figure in the background of her life and died when Elizabeth, the oldest of her eleven children, was twenty-two. It was Edward Moulton Barrett, one of the most formidable fathers who ever lived, who dominated his household and his favorite daughter. He was a domestic tyrant, benevolent only so long as his will was done. He did not wish any of his children, boys or girls, to escape from his thralldom. He discouraged all of them from marrying, and when two of them did so—without his consent, perforce—he never spoke to or of them again.

Mr. Barrett's considerable fortune came from large Jamaican sugar plantations which did not require his presence. He had no occupation but his household. Elizabeth, the pretty and gifted eldest daughter, was his particular concern. When she precociously wrote a poem about the Battle of Marathon at the age of twelve, he paid to have fifty copies printed. Even at this early age, the girl was proficient in Latin and Greek and loved the classics, which had a great influence on her own writing. Her first commercially published work (when she was twenty-seven) was a translation of *Prometheus Bound* from the Greek of Aeschylus.

Elizabeth had never been robust, but when she was fifteen she entered upon the life of invalidism to which she dedicated herself like a novice entering a convent. She had fallen from her pony, injuring her spine severely, and while abed developed a weakness in the lungs. In those days, invalids resigned themselves to inaction and sought relief in changes of air or climate. Elizabeth Barrett went to the seaside, accompanied by her favorite brother and close companion, Edward, the eldest of the Barrett boys. He was tragically drowned while sailing and her feeling of guilt—she considered herself responsible—almost killed her. She literally withdrew from the world.

By this time the family had moved from the country to London. The abolition of slavery in the West Indian colonies had made sugar planting far less profitable than it had been, with depressing but not disastrous effect on Mr. Barrett's fortune. He still had enough to live comfortably, if not luxuriously, in the house on Wimpole Street. Here Elizabeth had her own large bed-sitting-room upstairs, which she never left.

Although she did not go out into the world, she began sending out her poems, which were published in books and in various magazines, bringing her to the attention of literary men and women. She was written to and called upon by such figures as Walter Savage Landor, of "Rose Aylmer" fame, Leigh Hunt, who wrote "Abou Ben Adhem," and the great Wordsworth. Her father permitted her, when she felt strong enough, to receive visitors, lying on a chaise in her room, surrounded by her books and letters and kept company by her cocker spaniel, Flush.

Elizabeth Barrett was small, slight, frail and delicate, with large, dark eyes, a fine brow and dark brown hair worn like Flush's ears, hanging looped along either cheek in the current style. She wrote voluminous letters and read a great deal. She admired the works of Robert Browning, particularly "Pippa Passes." Browning's name first appeared in her correspondence in 1844, when she was thirty-eight. "Mr. Browning is said to be learned in Greek, especially the dramatists," she wrote to her friend Miss Mitford. That was something she and Mr. Browning had in common.

One day in January, 1845, she found in her mail a letter in an unfamiliar hand. It began with the words, "I love your verses with all my heart, dear Miss Barrett—and this is no offhand complimentary letter I shall write . . ." It went on,

Excerpts from GREAT LOVES IN LEGEND AND LIFE. Reprinted by permission of Curtis Brown, Ltd. Copyright © 1964 by Gwen Davenport.

"Since the day last week when I first read your poems, I quite laugh how I have been turning and turning again in my mind what I should be able to tell you of their effect upon me...into me it has gone, and part of me it has become, this great living poetry of yours, not a flower of which but took root and grew..."

The writer was Robert Browning.

Browning had reached the age of thirty-three without having given his heart to any woman. He had written of passionate love—but he had never been able to experience it. This was not because his nature was cold. He was a warm, human person, a thoroughly good man, and he had many friends. His conversation was brilliant and flowing. He was also an accomplished musician. Although his family was not wealthy, his kind and indulgent father had been willing for his son to attempt the financially hazardous career of a poet.

When this much-traveled man of the world addressed his first letter to the shut-in, he already had written several long dramatic poems and many of the shorter dramatic lyrics that are today his best-known works. These included "Home Thoughts from Abroad" (beginning, "Oh, to be in England now that April's here"), "Boot and Saddle," "The Lost Leader," "Incident of the French Camp" (ending, "Smiling, the boy fell dead"), "Childe Roland to the Dark Tower Came," and "The Pied Piper of Hamelin."

The first letter he sent to the upstairs room in Wimpole Street was answered the next day, at great length. The answer began, "I thank you, dear Mr. Browning, from the bottom of my heart...Such a letter from such a hand!" He had indicated a desire to call on her, and she wrote, "Winters shut me up as they do a dormouse's eyes; in the spring, we shall see..."

Two days later, he wrote again, and after that the letters flowed back and forth unceasingly until spring came and he reminded her, "...Real, warm spring, dear Miss Barrett, and the birds know it; and in spring I shall see you, surely see you—for when did I once fail to get whatever I had set my heart upon?" Again she put him off, then later asked, "Is it true that your wishes fulfill themselves? And when they do are they not bitter to your taste—do you not wish them unfulfilled?"

In the continuing correspondence that poured forth, the two spoke much of poetry and outside events, revealing themselves to one another through their observations and opinions. They also spoke directly of themselves and each other, explaining feelings and expressing gratitude, as when she wrote, "How kind you are!—how kindly and gently you speak to me! Although I am aware that you unconsciously exaggerate what I can be to you, yet it is delightful to be broad awake and think of you as my friend."

Before they even met, the friend of Elizabeth Barrett had begun to turn into the lover. Anxious inquiries about health were followed by earnest wishes to "see you with my own, own eyes." At last, in May, Browning wrote that if he could not see her he would leave London and travel. She told him to come.

His first visit lasted an hour and a half, and no one knows what was said. What happened, however, is well known. Robert Browning had already loved Elizabeth's spirit; now he loved her. He was thirty-three, handsome, robust and exuberantly vital. She was nearly forty and could not walk unassisted from her couch to her bed. She spoke of her poetry as the flower of herself. "...The rest of me is nothing but a root, fit for the ground and the dark..."

The extraordinary courtship went on for a year and a half under the nose of the unsuspecting Mr. Barrett, who had, so far successfully, discouraged any suitors in his house. Elizabeth had been allowed visitors, but it did not occur to her father that she would ever be courted, much less that she would herself fall in love. When first his invalid daughter began to go downstairs and then outdoors, he could not possibly imagine that she was trying her wings in trial flights as a preparation for quitting the nest. Her lover encouraged and sustained her, always pleading with her to marry him. Many times she said she could not listen to his love, for his own sake; she would not saddle him with an ailing wife. He overcame her every objection, and at last even persuaded her to disobey her father's unreasonable despotism.

In September, 1846, after weeks of plotting, the lovers were married secretly in St. Marylebone Church. Robert had obtained a special license, bought a ring, made arrangements with the minister and with a cousin who was to stand up with him. Elizabeth's only attendant and witness was her maid. No one in her numerous family was taken into her confidence, as she feared her father's vengeance on a brother or sister. Three minutes after the ceremony, bride and groom separated, the bride returning to Wimpole Street. There followed a week of planning and packing before the afternoon when Elizabeth, accompanied by the faithful maid carrying Flush, crept out of her father's house forever, to join her husband and go with him to Italy. The father never forgave.

A complete record of the Brownings' story exists in the letters each wrote to the other, which were published by their son many years after their deaths. The greatest collection of their letters and memorabilia is to be found, curiously not in London but in the Texas college town of Waco, at the Agricultural and Mechanical College. There were two sons born, one of whom did not live, and the marriage lasted happily for fifteen years. The two poets lived mostly in Italy, where the climate agreed with Mrs.

continued

Browning. Her husband always took devoted and tender care of her. She grew strong enough to travel, work and entertain. Both of them were always interested in liberal causes, to which they gave their time and talents; of money they never had more than just enough to live on decently.

An American friend, Mr. George Hillard, who knew the Brownings in Florence, wrote of them in his journal, "A happier home and a more perfect union than theirs it is not easy to imagine...A union so complete as theirs—in which the mind has nothing to crave nor the heart to sigh for—is cordial to behold and something to remember."

Letters were not the only writing Elizabeth Barrett had been doing in her room in Wimpole Street in the year before her marriage. She had composed fifty sonnets to her love, the last one completed only two days before the wedding. She did not mention their existence until she had been married for three years, when one day she handed Robert the manuscript and left him alone to read it.

The recipient needed no proof either of his wife's genius or of her love for him. The "Sonnets" told the world what the lover already knew. Being so personal, they were published anonymously as coming "from the Portuguese" as if they were translations from that language. Perhaps the most universally remembered of them is the next to last, written while she was trying to find the strength and courage to leave her life-in-death on Wimpole Street for life-in-love in Italy:

How do I love thee? Let me count the ways
I love thee to the depth and breadth and height
My soul can reach, when feeling out of sight
For the ends of Being and ideal Grace.
I love thee to the level of everyday's
Most quiet need, by sun and candlelight.
I love thee freely, as men strive for Right;
I love thee purely, as they turn from Praise.
I love thee with the passion put to use
In my old griefs, and with my childhood's faith.
I love thee with a love I seemed to lose
With my lost saints,—I love thee with the breath,
Smiles, tears, of all my life!—and, if God choose,
I shall but love thee better after death.

What lover would not want to be able to tell his beloved in words like these what he feels in his heart! Elizabeth Barrett Browning has done it for all lovers. Her sonnets transcend the purely personal to speak for everyone who has ever been in love. New editions continue to appear year after year, as new generations of lovers discover them. They will be read as long as the English language lives, as much because of who wrote them, and to whom they were written, as because they are great poetry.

Gwen Davenport

Escape me?
Never—
Beloved!
While I am I, and you are you,
So long as the world contains us both,
Me the loving and you the loth,
While the one eludes, must the other pursue.
My life is a fault at last, I fear:
It seems too much like a fate, indeed!
Though I do my best I shall scarce succeed.
But what if I fail of my purpose here?
It is but to keep the nerves at strain,
To dry one's eyes and laugh at a fall,
And, baffled, get up and begin again,—
So the chace takes up one's life, that's all.
While, look but once from your farthest bound
At me so deep in the dust and dark,
No sooner the old hope goes to ground
Than a new one, straight to the self-same mark,
I shape me—
Ever
Removed!

Robert Browning

If thou must love me, let it be for nought
Except for love's sake only. Do not say
'I love her for her smile—her look—her way
Of speaking gently, for a trick of thought
That falls in well with mine, and certes brought
A sense of pleasant ease on such a day'—
For these things in themselves, Beloved, may
Be changed, or change for thee,—and love, so wrought,
May be unwrought so. Neither love me for
Thine own dear pity's wiping my cheeks dry—
A creature might forget to weep, who bore
Thy comfort long, and lose thy love thereby!
But love me for love's sake, that evermore
Thou mayst love on, through love's eternity.

Elizabeth Barrett Browning

Madelyn Stanchfield Trebilcock

Pretty Peggy Vanderleet,
Gold head bent above her quilting,
Cross her small, slippered feet,
Thimble finger lightly tilting,
None would know to look to her
That her heart is all a-whir,
And that she can scarcely wait
The postman's whistle at the gate.

To My Sweet Valentine

Blue-eyed Peggy Vanderleet,
Stitching feather sprays through cotton,
Rose-bud lips pursed red and sweet,
Hoping one has not forgotten
That frail thing of airy grace
Hearts and flowers and paper lace,
Waiting with her eyes a-shine
For her lover's valentine.

Pink-cheeked Peggy Vanderleet
Hears three sudden shrill, high whistles!
Sheds her thimble, slippered feet
Flying like the down of thistles;
Flinging wide the door, and there—
Like an answer to a prayer
Like an answer to her hope,
Is the square, white envelope!

Darling Peggy Vanderleet,
Never through the coming hours
Will the postman bring as sweet
A gift, as this, of lace and flowers;
Never will your heart be quite
As fluttering and glad and light!
There is nothing quite as fine
As a girl's first valentine.

Grace Noll Crowell

*"A Valentine of Long Ago" from WHITE FIRE by Grace Noll Crowell. Copyright 1934
by Harper & Row, Publishers, Inc. Reprinted by permission of the publisher.*

The Valentine

Joy Belle Burgess

The valentine you gave to me
Is like a summer rose,
Aglow with all the warmth of love
And sweetness in each fold.

The treasured gift you gave to me
Is like a winter fire,
With words of love in thought and rhyme
That breathe of sweet desire.

The token fair you gave to me
Is like a spring bouquet,
Adorned with blue forget-me-nots
And ribbons bright and gay.

The valentine of frills and lace
Throughout the year will be
A most endearing gift because
You gave your love to me.

Love

With Love's chains thou hast bound me
    In sweet captivity,
A prisoner that despises
    All thought of liberty—
Ah, dear one, I've no craving
    From thy bondage to be free;
No desire no aspiration,
    Save thy vassal true to be.

Valentine's - A Day for All Ages

The air outside is brisk, and it will feel good to put an extra log on the fire tonight. Yet, there is a springlike brightness in the sunlight, and no one can help smiling at saucy cupid (surely "dressed" for summer) peaking out from a burst of flowers on the front of that charming card. Inside, no doubt in suitably elegant verse, is a message of true and everlasting affection.

Such warm greetings on a chilly day show that in the hearts of lovers everywhere there is no holiday so popular as February 14, Saint Valentine's Day. Who would believe that its origins are so wrapped in mystery? Yet, historical sources don't agree on many points, and on others there is only myth to turn to.

Celebration of Valentine's Day seems to have its roots in an ancient Roman festival of love held for the young people. When the Romans invaded Britain, they brought their festivals with them. Despite the rise of Christianity, the people continued to enjoy many pagan celebrations. Unable to eliminate the popular holiday, Christian priests determined to dedicate it to a Christian saint.

Saint Valentine was elected, authorities say, not because of any special connection with lovers, but because the date of his martyrdom happened to fall in mid-February. Myth has it, though, that during his imprisonment before execution he formed a friendship (fell in love) with the jailer's blind daughter, the only person who was kind to him. Just before his death he is said to have sent her a farewell message signed "From Your Valentino."

Centuries later, on February 14, it was the custom for marriageable young girls to place their names in an urn in a public square. Each eager young man then drew his "Valentine's" name from the urn in hopes of forming a permanent romance. In time an additional superstition grew up that the first unattached member of the opposite sex one saw on the morning of Saint Valentine's Day would be one's sweetheart for the year and, ultimately, one's husband or wife.

Somewhere along the line the idea of allowing fate to rule in matters of the heart became unpopular, and, whenever possible, people managed to "fix" the lottery or to see whomever they wished first in the morning. By the 1600s the whole thing had evolved into a very lighthearted festivity, and even children and married persons drew names and became valentines "at first sight" on that special day.

Up to that time the gentlemen had presented their valentines with gifts (sometimes extremely expensive ones), but unlike today there seem to have been no written valentine cards. During the seventeenth century people began bringing notes to those whose names they drew, with the valentine's name and a complimentary "Most Courteous and Fair," or other popular phrase, written decoratively on them.

In 1640, an interesting little book entitled *Cupid's Messenger* appeared. It was filled with verses that the inarticulate could turn to to help them express their amorous sentiments. Over the years a number of these "Valentine Writers" were published, and the tradition of writing poems for and about this lover's day has since been carried on by the best poets of the times as well as by those not so well known.

Few valentine love letters seem to have been mailed, perhaps because of the great cost and the fact that anything mailed to the country had to be picked up at the nearest inn. The usual practice was to leave the valentine at the sweetheart's door, knock, then dash away, out of sight.

Lover's greetings were not at first written on cards, but on full-size paper. However, in England and Europe it became the custom to write short greetings on visiting cards adorned with decorative borders or pictures. It was a natural step from the use of handwritten greeting cards to the use of specially printed ones.

By the 1780s cards in a multitude of styles were being published in England and Europe. Little winged cupids became popular as the central design of many. Cupid was, of course, notorious for striking humans with the arrows of love.

During the last part of the eighteenth century, the Germans contributed the *Freundeschaftskarten*—handmade friendship or lover's card—closely resembling the valentines of the next century. The Germans who settled in the United States during that century introduced this particular form of greeting, and its ornamental style spread to other parts of the country and influenced the American valentine which was beginning to become popular.

continued

Photograph Opposite (from top to bottom): Sourpuss valentine (Penny Dreadful, circa 1940s), Civil War valentine, Radio Bug valentine (Penny Dreadful, circa 1940s), Valentine postcard (Aurochrome series); all courtesy of Kean Archives.

Overleaf: Ornamental valentine and postcards, courtesy of Kean Archives; postcard "I never loved until . . . ," courtesy of Geraldine Zisk.

SOURPUSS

YOU'RE SUCH A GOL DERNED SOURPUSS
THAT I REALLY AM AFRAID
IF YOU STUCK YOUR FACE IN WATER
IT WOULD TURN TO LEMONADE!

Made in U.S.A

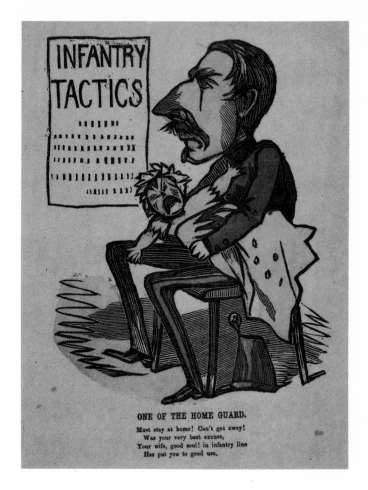

ONE OF THE HOME GUARD.

Must stay at home! Can't get away!
Was your very best excuse,
Your wife, good soul! in infantry line
Has put you to good use.

RADIO BUG

YOU PLAY THAT THING SO
GOL DERNED LOUD
YOU OUGHTA BE IN CHAINS!
HERE'S HOPING YOU BLOW
OUT YOUR TUBES
AND THEN . . . . BLOW
OUT YOUR BRAINS!

Made in U.S.A.

AURDR ROME SERIES, ALL RIGHTS RESERVED.

THE GROCER

You pose for a grocer so swell,
But we're on to you full well;
Your sugar's sand, and second-hand
Is all the stuff you sell.

Valentine
Think of Me

To Valentine

To my Valentine

I never loved until
I met you, sweet,
And now my heart is
pleading at your feet.

Early examples of lover's greetings were written with excellent penmanship and embellished with the writer's initials opposite those of his sweetheart. As in the early days of the written valentine in England, enterprising fellows who wrote with a fine hand probably found financially rewarding the penning of messages for the less gifted.

Flourishes of scrollwork, embellishments with water color, and the true-lover's knot were all popular. True-lover's knots took the form of a somewhat tangled-looking maze drawn on the card and filled with messages running each into the other and taking some time to follow to the end. These knots must have required almost as much time to decipher as to create!

"Puzzle Purses" were also well-liked. They were square envelopes, the four flaps of which were folded one inside the other. Each flap was doubled and perhaps decorated on both sides. Sometimes the puzzles contained a reward—a lock of hair or a ring. When one of them was opened the trick was not only to read the messages in the correct order, but also to fold all the flaps back up correctly.

Pin-pricked designs were rare and beautiful and found on cards sent by certain wealthy ladies with much leisure. The fancy border and the people on the card were pricked out by pins of varying thickness, giving an embossed effect.

Handmade and handwritten valentines prevailed in America for a time. By the 1840s, however, they had been replaced by manufactured ones.

In 1857 there were five firms making valentines in New York City. Cards were also imported from England, France, and Germany. Most were delicate lace paper creations of softly-tinted, finely-drawn bowers, lovers, and other symbolic figures of the 1850s. During the 1880s mechanical valentines were perfected. These were often constructed so that pulling tabs or decorative pieces revealed hidden messages.

Valentines in the next decade tended to be shiny, ornamental art work. Comic cards also flourished, although some had surfaced as early as the 1840s. The Aurochrome postcard series helped send uncomplimentary greetings to one's favorite grocer, broker, "autoist," or "freckled health food crank." Particularly popular were "Penny Dreadfuls," which featured insulting rhymes and unflattering sketches, meant just for those chums with well-developed senses of humor.

During World War I, lonesome servicemen were fond of a valentine which had a specially prepared surface on which the "girl of your dreams" could press her lips. Underneath the space, centered in the midst of a patriotic design, was the following verse:

A Kiss For You!

For Uncle Sam you're fighting,
And that makes me love you so
That I send a kiss in the space above
To take where'er you go.

It is the children, though, who have come closest to keeping the festive spirit of this day alive. Lovers have called Valentine's Day their own, but grade school girls and boys have continued to put together, with colored paper and glue, with tiny scissors and big hearts, those precious messengers of "I Love You" and "Be My Valentine" for moms and dads and teachers and friends. Most Americans can still remember carefully decorating old shoe boxes and cutting slits in the top. The day would seem forever, waiting and waiting...and then everyone would rush to the row of boxes to see what that special someone had to say.

And many a mom has surprised her young ones after school with another valentine. In fact, there were usually two or three, all heart-shaped and covered with pink icing and red cinnamon candies and accompanied by a big glass of ice cold milk.

Sending decorative valentines has been fairly widespread in recent years. Special gifts have also been developed for the occasion. Most everyone has been presented with one of those heart-shaped sugar lozenges with "I Love You," "Will You Be Mine?" or other message printed on it in vegetable dye. And many a wife or sweetheart has secretly hoped for one of those grand, red satin covered boxes filled with chocolates, peppermints, butter creams, or tiny red cinnamon hearts. Gift lines of children's books, jewelry, china, glassware and clothing make it easy to buy for dieters or other dear ones who cannot enjoy such delicacies.

Centuries after its beginnings, Valentine's Day is still celebrated. Gifts are bestowed on loved ones; handmade cards, created with love and painstaking attention, are presented to parents by eager school children; and lovers still choose with care the messengers of their affections. Its popularity may have faded for brief periods, but the joys of love and romance have kept Valentine's Day alive.

Norma L. Barnes

Please Be Mine, Valentine

Bea Bourgeois

I've often wondered if my lifelong fascination with mail didn't begin somewhere early in grade school, on Valentine's Day. There was always a delicious excitement hidden inside those small white envelopes—even when my name was printed backwards, misspelled, or smudged by the small fingers of my classmates.

Would I receive a card mysteriously signed "Billy A." from the most popular boy in the room? On the other hand, would the boy I considered "a drip" send me one? Wouldn't it be wonderful if they both did? And—although quality should have been more important than quantity—would I get as many cards as my best girlfriend got?

Valentine's Day generated a lot of fuss when I was a youngster. I attended a parochial grade school, and Valentine's Day usually fell close to or during Lent. As first and second graders, we looked forward to the frivolity and bright colors during an otherwise solemn and penitential season.

Beginning early in February, our class discussed the construction of the valentine mailbox. Someone's father always provided a large, square cardboard box that we decorated during Friday afternoon art classes.

Covered with red and white crepe paper and festooned with hearts, arrows, and cupids, the finished mailbox occupied a position of honor on a table at the front of the classroom. Red construction paper arrows pointed to the wide slot on top where, on February 14, we would deposit our personal stacks of mail.

At least a week before the day itself, my mother and I would make a special trip to the dime store to buy a box of colorful valentine cards—50 for 19 cents. Classes were larger in those days, and my hand often stiffened as I signed my name 35 or 40 times. I tried very hard to match the right card to the right classmate.

Messages on the "penny" valentines have remained fairly constant through the years. There is the tall, smiling giraffe on the front with a message inside proclaiming "Valentine, I long for you"; or a cowboy with red heart on his vest, swinging a lariat and announcing "Valentine, I'd like to steer you my

way!"; or a fat, red beet announcing, "Valentine, my heart beets for you!" We giggled at every one of those corny jokes, too.

There was always an impressive ceremony surrounding the delivery of valentine mail. Several of the children (usually those with impeccable marks in conduct and behavior) were chosen to be the "mailmen" with the accompanying honor of passing out cards to the rest of the class. Sister insisted on order: "We'll go by rows," she would say, and each mailman would deliver handsful of valentines to the nervous occupants of rows one through five.

Several Mothers had "volunteered" (actually, we did the volunteering) to provide cupcake and candy treats for the party that followed the mail delivery. I remember placing a small candy heart atop each cupcake my mother had baked for the festivities. Who would get the heart that said "Wow, Babe" on it? Or the one that said, in those days, "Hubba Hubba"? I probably ate two of the minty flavored hearts for every five that were plopped into the pink frosting.

Valentine's Day traditions haven't changed much over the years. The mailbox has been modernized from one large collection depot into individual brown sandwich bags, still decorated with hearts and cupids. Our boys have accepted the more modern trend, and happily tape their individual sack to the front of their desks. Some things don't change, though; Sister still insists on order, and the mail is delivered row by row.

I can't remember when we became embarrassed about sending valentines, but as a parent myself now I'd guess it's along about sixth or seventh grade. One's reputation is at stake, after all, and a great deal of teasing might result from sending a particular boy or girl a card that has been designated as "mushy."

Somewhere, though, deep in a dresser drawer or far back on a closet shelf, those crumpled brown paper bags have been saved from first grade on. They seem to be a corner of childhood that we're all reluctant to part with—a silly or sentimental time when we could ask each and every classmate to "Please Be Mine, Valentine."

Early American Dolls
The Rag Doll

Perhaps the most common of the "home-made" dolls in the early years of American history were those made of rags—literally scraps from the rag bag. Torso, arms and legs were made of rolled cloth and stitched. Heads were stuffed with cotton or bits of cloth. Nose, mouth and eyebrows were sketched with pencil or ink, and eyes often came out of the button box. Fruit juices were sometimes used to add color to cheeks and lips.

When Jean Canaday attempted to wash the face of what she is sure is a doll from the Conestoga wagon days (found in a trunk in the attic of an old barn in Ohio), she discovered that the threads were loose, so she slipped the face off—like a mitten from a child's hand. To her surprise, another face appeared under it. Further investigation disclosed a third face under the second. All were sketched with pencil. It seems that when one face became stained or the features faded, the mother just made another and slipped it over the old one, stitching it in place.

The old rag dolls were first flat-faced and of all sizes and shapes. Many of the very old American rag dolls were lost in caravans, floods and other disasters.

When the sewing machine was invented, rag dolls could be made faster and were sturdier. The strong woven fabrics such as muslin were best, but eventually non-woven or felted fabrics were used for dolls also.

In 1855, a woman named Izannah F. Walker made rag dolls that are now sought out by collectors. Eventually—about 1873—this woman patented a process by which cloth could be pressed into molds in the desired doll head form, treated to hold its shape and painted with oils.

About 1890, Emma Adams originated a special kind of rag doll in Oswego, New York. She entered one of these creations which she named "Miss Columbia" at the Chicago World's Fair in 1893, for which she won a diploma of merit. Miss Adams' rag dolls (or cloth dolls) had nicely shaped bodies and heads, oil-painted hair and features; and she took great care in making their clothes according to the style of the day.

In 1900, "Miss Columbia" was selected as queen of the International Doll Collection to tour the United States, and later the world, for children's charities. (The collection was owned by Miss Elizabeth R. Horton of Boston, Massachusetts at the time, and it was she who was responsible for the tour.) On the world trip, "Miss Columbia" was mentioned by journalists in the news as "the gem of all rag dolls," "America's doll"—destined to become the most famous doll in the world. No Adams dolls were made after the death of their creator in 1908.

A novel rag doll (also in my collection) has a dual personality. Made of cloth and stuffed with cotton, the doll has two heads and torsos that are fastened together at the waistline. Each doll has her own bodice, of course, but a common skirt (double thickness) that covers the torso and head of one doll, when tucked down into place. If a child should tire of the brunette with the brown yarn hair, she could flip the skirt over the doll's head and there she would find a blonde with hair of yellow yarn. The brunette dressed all in blue, wears an expression of serenity, while the blonde, dressed in pink, has an 0-shaped mouth, wide-open eyes and raised eyebrows, giving her an expression of perpetual surprise. (Faces are embroidered.) Two dolls in one!

This doll has an unknown origin, having been in my family for years, handed down from generation to generation.

However, according to Ilse Gray, she may be quite old. Gray says, "In the middle of the 19th century doll manufacturers began to produce various kinds of mechanical and novelty dolls...At about the same time, dolls with two heads—one at either end of the body—became popular. These had a wide skirt attached to the waist which served to hide whatever head was at the bottom."

The author writes that some such dolls were based on the "rags and riches" theme, while some had a black doll at one end and a white one at the other.

After a time, the making of rag dolls at home was made easier by an imaginative manufacturer who conceived the idea of printing fabric with a front and back image of a doll, sold over the counter at dry goods stores. The buyer cut around the figure on the dotted line and sewed front and back together, stuffing the dolls with cotton. Some of the figures represented pretty little girls with curls and hair ribbons or good-looking little boys; however, some manufacturers printed images of well-known cartoon and story book characters such as Goldilocks, Little Red Riding Hood, Buster Brown and his dog Tige, and Aunt Jemima.

Dolls have been used through the years to advertise products. One of the earliest known is a cloth boy doll distributed to promote the Boston Cash Register Company in the early 1800s.

Dolls made of cloth may still be purchased in toy stores because they can be soft and cuddly—the kind small children like to take to bed with them—and because they are durable.

Quoting Ilse Gray again, "A cloth doll can last several generations, as it did in the family of Mrs. Martha Reed of Kalamazoo, Michigan. Mrs. Reed made a doll called Aggie in 1851, and Aggie has lived in the Reed family for four generations. Her hair is made of floss and her features are embroidered."

Two of the long-time favorite rag dolls are of course Raggedy Ann and her counterpart, Raggedy Andy. Popularity of these early 20th century dolls has been phenomenal. According to an article in the PLAIN DEALER (Cleveland, Ohio), Raggedy's creator was Johnny Gurelle of Silvermine, Connecticut, a cartoonist, illustrator and writer. According to the article, the stories around Raggedy Ann were based on his daughter Marcella (who died at the age of 14 in 1916).

According to the story in the Raggedy books, a little girl found a rag doll in the attic with brown eyes and a mop of hair. Whether or not this is true, the writer of the article says it was known that a doll was found in the attic of the Guerelle home and a new face was painted on it. It was this doll after which the Raggedys were modeled. It is believed the first doll went on the market about 1918.

After the popularity of these lovable dolls was established, patterns for making them at home were put on the market. Unfortunately, the pattern has changed somewhat over the years. Some doll makers follow suggestions on the patterns and embroider the eyes; however in the original, eyes were represented by big round shiny buttons.

Raggedy Andy dolls were usually dressed in a shirt with Buster Brown collar and tie, short pants with two buttons in front, and a cap topping the mop of yellow hair. Raggedy Ann usually appeared in a colorful little print dress with a white apron. Faces of the two are similar with a wide smile, large eyes, raised eyebrows, and a triangle for a nose.

The Raggedys—like other cloth dolls—are passed from mother to daughter . . . down the line, as favorites for small children.

Doris A. Paul

Mommy's Valentine

You're Mommy's little angel
As precious as can be,
Not very big, that's certain,
But all the world to me.
I love you, little darling,
I'm very glad you're mine,
So once again, I tell you
You're Mommy's valentine.

You're Mommy's little laddie,
A big important part
Of every new tomorrow,
You've stolen Mommy's heart;
No one could ever doubt it
You're all that's dear and fine,
A treasured little sweetheart,
You're Mommy's valentine.

How very fast you're growing,
So soon the time will come
When someone else will steal the heart
Of Mommy's precious son;
Give her your love, my darling,
But promise through all time,
That I shall always rate a kiss
From Mommy's valentine.

Garnett Ann Schultz

From Daddy's Girl

Daddy is my valentine.
I know that Daddy's heart is mine.
I love to sit on Daddy's knee
While he sings silly songs to me.
Sometimes we go for a walk
Just so he and I can talk;
He says I'm made of sugar and spice
And I think Daddy's very nice.
He calls me princess all the time,
The best Daddy in the world is mine!

Marla Heim

Love Is a Gift of God

Love is a gift of God. It is far more precious than any
material thing one could ever hope to possess. It can't be
purchased, for along with all of the best things in life, it is
free. Its magic can change a dreary world into a heaven on
earth. Its radiance is beyond human power of description. It
is not restricted by race, creed or public opinion and has
nothing to do with physical appearance, for "beauty is in the
eye of the beholder." There is no fault or shortcoming that
love cannot overcome with charity and understanding. It
does not imprison, but rather, in loving, one is set free.
There is no limit to what love can accomplish, for its depth
finds qualities that would otherwise remain undiscovered. It
is the most beautiful, the most absorbing, and the most
rewarding thing in life and by far the most important. For
love is truly a gift of God.

Dorothy Bettencourt Elfstrom

The Owl and the Pussy-Cat

The Owl and the Pussy-Cat went to sea
   In a beautiful pea-green boat:
They took some honey, and plenty of money
   Wrapped up in a five-pound note.

The Owl looked up to the stars above,
   And sang to a small guitar,
"O lovely Pussy! O Pussy, my love,
   What a beautiful Pussy you are,
     You are, you are!
What a beautiful Pussy you are!"

Pussy said to the Owl, "You elegant fowl!
   How charmingly sweet you sing!
O let us be married! too long we have tarried:
   But what shall we do for a ring?"

They sailed away for a year and a day,
   To the land where the Bong tree grows,
And there in a wood a Piggy-wig stood,
   With a ring at the end of his nose,
     His nose, his nose,
   With a ring at the end of his nose.

"Dear Pig, are you willing to sell for one shilling
   Your ring?" Said the Piggy, "I will."
So they took it away, and were married next day
   By the Turkey who lives on the hill.

They dined on mince, and slices of quince,
   Which they ate with a runcible spoon;
And hand in hand, on the edge of the sand,
   They danced by the light of the moon,
     The moon, the moon,
   They danced by the light of the moon.

Edward Lear

Winter Delight

The land wears a robe of white velvet,
  All braided and trimmed with lace;
Each tiny limb in ermine trim
  Bows in silent grace.

The snow robe is threaded in crystal,
  In sparkle and glitter and gleam;
Great white flakes fall in wonder
  Like the charm of a mystic dream.

The everyday world is perfection,
  For the storm that came last night,
Brought snow in its regal beauty
  For children's intrigued delight.

Mamie Ozburn Odum

A Dreamer's Snowfall

A song is in the snowfall,
  A bird of soft, white wings,
A little winter dreaming,
  The world of children's things.

A hush is in the forest,
  A carpet in the hills;
It seems as if time's stopping
  And talking to windmills.

A God is in the snowfall,
  The God of peaceful homes;
The shy deer stops to notice,
  The trees are silver poems.

A beauty's in the snowfall,
  A Cinderella's shoe,
It's like a picture postcard,
  A world that's bright and new!

Marion Schoeberlein

The Little Girl Next Door

The little girl who lives next door
   Has hair of fluffy brown;
And when she walks beside me
   The curls bounce up and down.

Her eyes have twinkles in them,
   They're dancing all the while;
And when she speaks to me, I see
   The dimples in her smile.

Her leggings button at the side,
  She has a coat with fur;
And one day when it snowed, I put
  Her rubbers onto her.

I'm saving all my pennies now
  To buy her something fine;
I saw it in a window—
  It's a fancy valentine.

It's made of hearts and paper lace,
  It costs a dime or more.
But nothing is too fine to give
  The little girl next door!

Helen Wing

Winter's Wealth

Winter's wealth is found in beauty.
   It hangs on all the trees;
It blankets earth with whiteness,
   And mirrors lakes that freeze.

It delights the mountain skiers,
   Brings the sleigh bells out;
It decorates the playgrounds
   With snowmen, round and stout.

For those who stay inside their homes
   With hearthfires as their goals,
The soft glow from a burning log,
   Gives wealth unto their souls.

Adelaide Blanton

Winter Memories

In winter, I remember still...
(As bundled youngsters trudge uphill
With sleds behind them, lagging there,
As snowflakes drift through pathless air—

And when atop the hill they rest
Just wondering which snow-trail is best,)
I seem to see myself in them
As I relive old scenes again!

It seems that wintertime is fun—
But somehow only, to the young!
For as the years creep up on me—
My rocking chair seems best, you see!

The snowball fights seemed quite the thing
For fingers cold, from winter's sting.
And games were always fun, you know,
Like making "Angels," in the snow.

A dish of snow "ice-cream" was good
Beside the stove—made warm with wood.
And icicles hanging from the eaves
And diamonds glistening from the trees

Were things of beauty, given free
To the likes of you and me!
The curling smoke from chimneys, tall,
Lent a sense of serenity over all.

Yes, wintertime is fun, no doubt
To youngsters who can run about,
But give me warmth, and books, galore—
And my rocking chair—why ask for more!

Beatrice Drummond

Winter Morning

What magic has been wrought o'ernight,
  That the blue dawning wakes
A snow-white world, a fairy scene,
  Of crystaled trees and lakes?

High-piled the snow on field and path,
  So deeply lying covered,
That where the walk ends, or the road,
  Can scarcely be discovered.

A crystal bridge the brooklet spans,
  Blue ice and drifted snow.
The trees shake starry blossoms down
  Whene'er the wind doth blow.

Asleep, the violet in her snowy bed;
  Dreaming, the wild rose vine;
Still, lies the fairy white world;
  Soft breathes the sighing pine.

Ruth L. Nine

From Loveland with Love

Dan Cupid isn't partial,
His darts fly everywhere.
So let your heart be target,
For one with love to share..
Loveland, Colorado

Why not add a special sentimental touch to Valentine's Day this year by sending a valentine to your sweetheart via "The Valentine Capitol of the World?" And better yet, how about convincing your sweetheart to send you one in return? Sound like a sweet idea? Well, the residents of Loveland, Colorado and the thousands of people who send valentine letters there every year will gladly tell you just how sweet it is.

The custom of remailing valentines from Loveland, Colorado, "The Sweetheart Town," originated many years ago with those romantics who felt the Loveland postmark added something unique to their valentine messages. Not until 1947, however, did anyone consider officially establishing and publicizing the service. At that time, the resident cupids—Postmaster Elmer Ivers and President of the Loveland Chamber of Commerce, Ted Thompson—decided to spread the spirit of Valentine's Day by improving and expanding the service.

Realizing that the valentine letters required something more elaborate than just the post-mark, Ivers and Thompson added a crimson cachet consisting of a four-line verse, an outline of the Rocky Mountains (those majestic peaks that lie directly to the west of the city), and topped off by Loveland's very own Cowboy Cupid. This version of the mischievous Roman god of love came complete with boots, ten-gallon Stetson, chaps, and was usually armed with a bow and arrow, occasionally westernized into a lariat. Each successive year, Thompson worked with his wife to develop a new idea and theme for another original verse and a slightly modified design, thereby changing the cachet every year for the benefit of collectors.

Already in its thirty-third consecutive year, the project has thus far received a great response; the number of letters has snowballed from a few hundred in 1947 to nearly 200,000 last year. Over the past two years the heaviest volume of mail has arrived from Charlotte, North Carolina, along with a substantial amount of letters from St. Louis, Missouri. Elementary school classes send quite a few valentines, as do savings and loan firms, gift shops, retail stores, and radio stations, primarily for promotional purposes. In addition, the service is used as a method of contacting celebrities in every field, from entertainment and sports to politics and government to royalty. Some of the users of the service live as far away as Tokyo, Mexico City, and Rome, or as nearby as Denver and Cheyenne.

Although Elmer Ivers has retired, the present postmaster, together with his crew, handles the avalanche of valentine mail quickly, carefully, and efficiently, remailing it to all of the fifty states and to most foreign countries as well. Consequently, in appreciation for all his efforts, the postmaster himself receives somewhere between 6,000 and 8,000 valentine letters and cards that simply say, "Thank you." Fortunately, he can always count on the help offered annually by at least thirty to forty retirees who volunteer to brand every valentine with the cachet as a "labor of love."

Of the thousands of people who value the remailing service, no one values it more than Lovelanders. Besides putting their mountain metropolis on the world map, and adding to its already booming reputation as a gateway to the Rockies, the great success of the project has given Loveland's citizens a real sense of community and self-identity; Valentine's Day has become their own special holiday, rivaling Easter, Christmas, and even rodeo time. Their observance of this national day for sweethearts even includes the selection of a Miss Loveland Valentine, a high school senior girl, chosen by the student bodies of the high schools, and interviewed by a panel of citizens. Miss Valentine acts as Loveland's goodwill ambassador, representing the city at banquets and other formal affairs, and visiting shut-ins and residents of nursing homes. Loveland's daughters consider it, indeed, an honor to represent their city at the most important event of the year in Loveland.

So why not give Valentine's Day a little more importance on your calendar by participating in this long distance game of "post office." Should you decide to do so, please address valentine letters (including the zip code) and affix proper postage to each. Place them in an envelope, container, or outer wrapper addressed to:

> The Postmaster
> Attention: Valentines
> Loveland, Colorado 80537

The postmaster suggests sending them via first class mail far enough in advance to ensure arrival in Loveland by February 7. If you do not specify a particular mailing date, the letters will be remailed from Loveland February 9 or 10, depending on the distance they must travel. To ensure delivery to the receiver by February 14, mail addressed to foreign countries must arrive in Loveland several days earlier than February 7.

Give your sweetheart, your friends, and yourself a treat with Cowboy Cupid's personal valentine message from Loveland with love.

Beverly Rae Wiersum

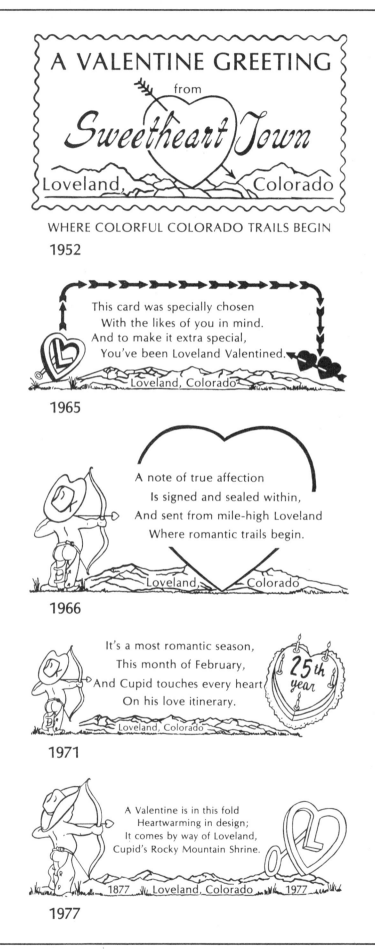

February

All outdoors
Edged in lace,
Twigs and grasses . . .
Beauteous grace.

Sunlight glows
Through snowy birches,
On frosty limb
A blue jay perches.

Thank you, Lord,
For heavenly art,
Your valentine
Has touched my heart.

Adeline Roseberg

A. LINCOLN

February Greetings

February is the bridge
On which we cross to spring.
When pendants hang like lovely jewels
And soft, warm snowflakes cling
To bushes, trees, roofs and eaves,
In dazzling display . . .
To tempt the weary traveler,
To cherish and delay!

George L. Ehrman

Butternut Wisdom

Gladys Taber

Although winter's moods prevail at Stillmeadow, a brief thaw makes us dream of spring, and Valentine Day brightens the month with its hearts-and-flowers

February is a chancy month in New England. It is a month when Nature herself seems now and then to be tired of the eternal cold and endless storms. Then we have the February thaw, and no matter how much we know, we firmly believe it is spring when the thaw gentles the land. There is the lovely sound of running water as ice and snow melt and brooks break loose. There is an open place in the middle of the dark glassy pond.

Then we are back in winter. The wind sounds as if this were Wuthering Heights, and snow and sleet fall from a low flat sky. The winter birds blow about like leaves, and need extra helpings of heat-giving food. What snow had melted on the road glazes over, so a trip to the village is an impossibility, no matter how often Holly urges it. Hal Borland tells me the Indians called this "the hunger moon," and it seems fitting. My hunger is for spring and wide-open roads and a car with an unfrozen windshield.

During the last severe storm I decided to take a whole day of rest. I wasn't, I decided, going to do a single thing but rest and read. Kind of a house vacation. I began very well by staying in bed late. Of course, I had to get up at eight to let Holly out, and again at 8:30 to let her back in, her fur all fringed with snow and sleet. But after I toweled her dry, I went back to bed. Then I got up and fixed a good breakfast of French toast, baby sausages, cranberry juice, and coffee. So far, it seemed a fine program. Then I had to build the fire up, and this involved taking out the ashes, which in turn involved cleaning the floor because a lot of them sifted over it.

Then I settled down to read "The Blue Lantern," by Colette, reading as slowly as possible to savor every crystalline word (but I cannot read slowly). In about an hour I had more coffee and noted that the coffeepot needed cleaning. Somehow this reminded me of another chore—defrosting my refrigerator. Then I washed the kitchen floor because it had melted ice flakes all over it. By then the dogs were ready for a run and a snack. The birds were ready for more food, too. So I got us all fed.

I really cannot say how I found myself cleaning out the fireplace cupboard in my room. It reminds me of a wornout stuffed toy that, at the slightest touch, sends the insides all over the room. This particular cupboard is lined with the kind of old plaster that is made of sand and hair, and a good deal of it sifts out on the rug when I open the door. So I had to get out my worst enemy, the vacuum cleaner. I am always on the wrong side of the hose, but that is only one problem.

By suppertime I fixed a pickup meal and watched Huntley and Brinkley. And thus ended my day of complete rest, and it had been very wearing! But as I had theoretically rested all day, I felt I should really work at the typewriter a couple of hours. And this involved putting in a new ribbon. I hope changing a typewriter ribbon is just a personal disaster for me and not a general one. I am always covered with ink, and yards of old ribbon spiral under the bed, and the new ribbon—resisting to the end—runs backward and stops, leaving extra loops hanging down on the keyboard.

There is no excuse for this, for I have been typing since I was 14. My typewriter is my dearest friend and constant companion. If I ever write a note by hand to the family, I get an immediate response. They call me up to ask what I said and why hadn't I typed it. So it is only the ribbon that is my enemy. Usually I keep using the old one until my son-in-law or Val turns up and I work the conversation around until it seems natural to say, "As long as you are here, would you mind..."

Finally, worn out with my day of rest, I went to bed and decided I would finish "The Blue Lantern" the next day while I ran the clothes washer.

This month brings Valentine Day, and I love it. It is such a romantic and sentimental holiday—all pink and blue and lacy. It is for the young and also for the young in spirit. I remember it was the one time of year when Father spent money on flowers or a plant for Mamma. He thought it was pretty silly, but he always gave in and bought her something he was told would keep well, and then he was furious because it didn't last for weeks. "Waste of money!" he snorted.

But Mamma used to save a leaf or two and tuck them in a book. It was a nice change from the presents he usually gave her—such as "The History of the Cheyenne Indians," which he wanted. Father wished to put his money into worthwhile things.

On a moon-filled night I go out on the terrace to look at the sky, remembering this is the same sky that since 1690 has curved above Stillmeadow and was there long before. The permanence of the sky is a wondrous thing to contemplate in this troubled age. It is never the same—sometimes soft and tender in summer, clashing with black clouds during a hurricane, pewter on a snowy day. Sometimes small bunny clouds leap across it as if it were a blue meadow; and sometimes, as now, it is like black glass with the moon a fresh-water pearl dropped on it. But it is always there, infinite, for men to lift their eyes to. I lift mine and wait for the cold silver light to catch in the ebon branch of the tallest sugar maple. And my heart knows the earth is turning toward spring, even now, even this bitter night.

The Cardinal

Little pine twig took to bouncing
   As its method of announcing
     That a visitor had
       landed on its snow.
There, defying wintery weather
   Was a puff of bright red feather
     Like a symbol of the courage
       he must know.

Then he gave the world an earful
   Of a song so sweet and cheerful
     That it seemed the garden
       ought to come awake;
But I'm sure he knew it wouldn't—
   Knew his efforts simply couldn't
     Melt the frosting on
       a February cake.

Still he sang with all his being
   Til he really had me seeing
     There against the lacy
       background of the pine
One small scarlet heart a-beating
   As for someone's heart competing.
     What a lovely little
       living valentine!

Margaret Rorke

Lake Atitlan, Lake of Love

Lake Atitlan, located in the central highlands of southwestern Guatemala, is spectacularly beautiful, but changeable, fickle, and sometimes stormy and dangerous to all who venture out upon its waters. These characteristics might be responsible for its name, Atitlan, composed of two parts: "ati," meaning water or lake, and "lin," meaning love. Lake of Love.

Coming upon it suddenly, after a hair-raising drive around sharp, hazardous curves on the mountain roads, was a breathtaking experience. A gem set in a valley dammed by volcanic ash. Clouds floated lightly in horizontal layers among the peaks of the volcanoes etched against the delicate coloring of the sky. The scene presented the perfect study for an exquisite fine-brush Japanese painting.

The three volcanoes, San Lucas Toliman, Santiago-Atitlan and San Pedro, "dip their feet" into the lake, said by the Mayan Indians in the area to be bottomless—that it "goes through the end of the world." (Authorities estimate the depth to be 1260 feet.) San Lucas Toliman has two heads, giving the basis for the oft-made statement that four volcanoes, rather than three, stand guard over the precious lake. Waters of many rivers feed into Atitlan, which is about sixteen miles in length, but drainage is undergound.

Borrowing a description of Lake Atitlan from Joan Lloyd, author of *Guatemala, Land of the Mayas,* "Sometimes waters are cerulean, so blue you can think of nothing but sapphires and hyacinth and blue love-in-a-mist growing among its feathery leaves; sometimes they are as gray-green as the Atlantic on a winter's day; sometimes almost black, when thunder clouds are rolling overhead." On that particular day, Lake Atitlan was a sapphire.

As I stood high above the lake, overwhelmed by its beauty, I was told that twelve Indian villages are rooted on its shores, each one named for one of the twelve apostles. However, since that day I have been led to doubt that statement, for one authority writes that there are less than twelve, one carrying the name Santa Cruz. However, the charm of this legend still remains, for we know of villages that garland the shore named San Marco, San Pablo, San Pedro, San Juan, and Santiago.

Centuries ago the Tzutuhile Maya people established a well fortified stronghold on the promontory that reaches out into the lake between the volcanoes Santiago-Atitlan and San Pedro. A powerful tribe, they boasted a large fleet of war canoes, and their domination of the lake was unquestioned. However, after a Spanish invasion, the power of the ruling family, called "House of the Eagle," was shattered, and life on and around Atitlan underwent many great changes.

Now Mayan Indians inhabiting the area earn their living through fishing, weaving cotton and woolen textiles, and harvesting some of the world's best coffee on the high volcanic slopes.

After leaving mirror-like Atitlan, my companions and I drove to our hotel, aptly named Casa Contente, in the village of Panajachel. The following day we took a motor launch across the lake to Santiago de Atitlan to visit the Indian woman's market. We discovered the shoreline to be irregular with little coves where the women washed their clothes and children played. Little gray lava "shavings," washed down the mountainside, bobbed on the water licking the shore.

Fascinated by the colorful market, the women wearing their unique halo-like headdresses fashioned of multihued ribbon, the sixteenth century church, its sanctuary adorned with strange, primitive —almost grotesque—wood carvings of the Holy Family, we were loathe to leave Santiago. At the repeated urgings of our guide we finally boarded the launch.

It was not long before we understood why he had been concerned about our delay in departure. The water, so serene when we crossed, had changed its mood to anger, kicking up the surface into deep furrows. We experienced the furor of the "chocomil," the giant afternoon wind that comes whistling down the mountains at almost the same time every day, churning the waters unmercifully. We were told that the native Mayans have learned to bring their canoes safely to shore before it descends. We were deeply grateful to set foot on solid ground after a very stormy crossing.

And so, Lake Atitlan, Lake of Love, considered by many world travelers to be the most beautiful in the world, commands a feeling of great admiration and awe, but also a deep respect for its changing moods that can imperil the lives of those foolish enough to challenge it.

Doris A. Paul

Valentine
ISSUE

ideals

Ideals' Pages
from the Past

On the following pages
we are presenting a selection
from Valentine Ideals 1952.

A Holiday

Lucile Coleman

When sweethearts meet, music should play.
When sweethearts meet, their hearts should be gay.
For life is sweet, true love is rare,
And time is fleet beyond compare.

When sweethearts meet, across their path
Moonbeams should spread a silvery bath.
The stars overhead should light love's way,
For life is complete, a holiday —
When sweethearts meet.

Dreams of Long Ago

Henry B. Knox

When, long ago in boyhood's days
I dreamt of joys untold,
With all the things that wealth would buy
As years would soon unfold;
I dreamt of one, who like a star
Before me seemed to shine, —
A girl of fifteen years or so, —
My Love, — my Valentine.

I'd build for her a castle fair
With gardens all around,
With lawns of green, and trellises
Where vines like ribbons wound
About the lattice-work above,
Bright colors to combine,
And 'neath its shade I'd meet her there, —
My Love, — my Valentine.

I dreamt of countries we would see
In journeys far and wide,
And all the joys I'd share with her
When trav'ling by my side;
From Scotland's lakes and heathered hills
To castles on the Rhine,
With her they'd seem more beautiful; —
My Love, — my Valentine.

And then in some secluded spot
We'd have our Country home,
Where through the forest aisles we'd stroll
And o'er the hills we'd roam, —
Beside the brooks and waterfalls
In summer time we'd dine,
And birds would sing their songs for her, —
My Love, — my Valentine.

Then chide me not for boyhood's dreams, —
My "Castles in the air",
For just to dream is often sweet
And always free from care;
But if I owned the world, and all
Its luxuries so fine,
They'd be a dowry far too small
For her, — my Valentine.

But now life's span seems short to me, —
The years have marked their score
Upon my brow, yet still I love
To dream the old dreams o'er,
For 'round my heart, like threads of gold
Their recollections twine
As by my side I see my wife, —
My Love, — my Valentine.

We know the joys of wedded life, —
We've tasted sorrows too,
And faith in God has never failed
To take us safely through;
Yet though the years may take their toll,
That girl of old lang syne
Is still to me, and e'er shall be
My Love, — my Valentine!

To One I Love

Eleanor Hillemann

I can think of nothing better
Than the years ahead with you;
Of walking down the path of life,
And making dreams come true.

I can think of nothing sweeter
Than to have you by my side,
To cherish you forever,
And in your heart abide.

There's a precious bit of heaven
In your eyes whene'er you smile,
And it makes me very happy
Just to be with you the while.

I can hear the angels singing
When you whisper words of love,
And I thank my God in Heaven
For His precious gift of love.

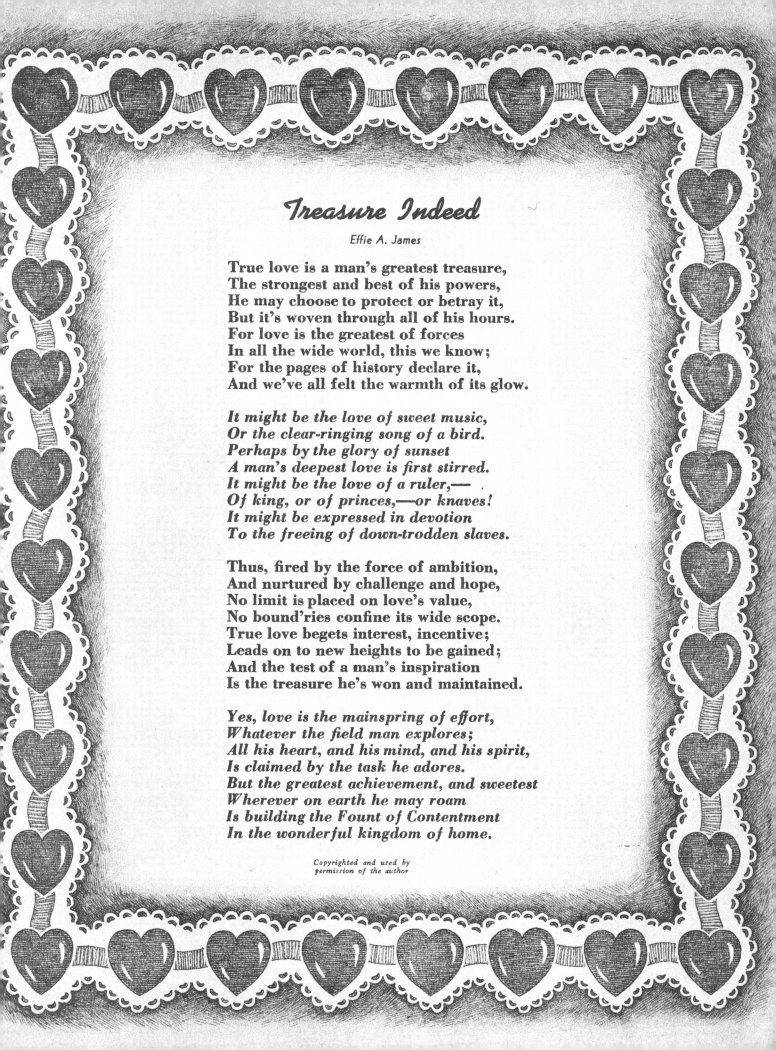

Treasure Indeed

Effie A. James

True love is a man's greatest treasure,
The strongest and best of his powers,
He may choose to protect or betray it,
But it's woven through all of his hours.
For love is the greatest of forces
In all the wide world, this we know;
For the pages of history declare it,
And we've all felt the warmth of its glow.

It might be the love of sweet music,
Or the clear-ringing song of a bird.
Perhaps by the glory of sunset
A man's deepest love is first stirred.
It might be the love of a ruler,——
Of king, or of princes,——or knaves!
It might be expressed in devotion
To the freeing of down-trodden slaves.

Thus, fired by the force of ambition,
And nurtured by challenge and hope,
No limit is placed on love's value,
No bound'ries confine its wide scope.
True love begets interest, incentive;
Leads on to new heights to be gained;
And the test of a man's inspiration
Is the treasure he's won and maintained.

Yes, love is the mainspring of effort,
Whatever the field man explores;
All his heart, and his mind, and his spirit,
Is claimed by the task he adores.
But the greatest achievement, and sweetest
Wherever on earth he may roam
Is building the Fount of Contentment
In the wonderful kingdom of home.

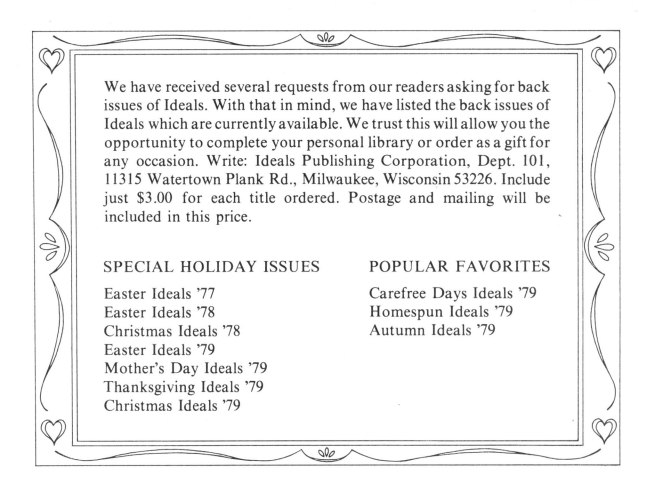

We have received several requests from our readers asking for back issues of Ideals. With that in mind, we have listed the back issues of Ideals which are currently available. We trust this will allow you the opportunity to complete your personal library or order as a gift for any occasion. Write: Ideals Publishing Corporation, Dept. 101, 11315 Watertown Plank Rd., Milwaukee, Wisconsin 53226. Include just $3.00 for each title ordered. Postage and mailing will be included in this price.

SPECIAL HOLIDAY ISSUES

Easter Ideals '77
Easter Ideals '78
Christmas Ideals '78
Easter Ideals '79
Mother's Day Ideals '79
Thanksgiving Ideals '79
Christmas Ideals '79

POPULAR FAVORITES

Carefree Days Ideals '79
Homespun Ideals '79
Autumn Ideals '79

ACKNOWLEDGMENTS

SNIP, SNIP . . . SCHERENSCHNITTE by R. A. Baumgart. Copyrighted and used by permission of the author. HEARTS OLD AND NEW by Ruth B. Field, from *Keepsakes.* Used with permission. THE BUGGY RIDE; THE LANGUAGE OF FLOWERS; THE PARLOR SOFA; THE VALENTINE, from *LOVE AND COURTSHIP IN AMERICA,* copyrighted, permission by Hastings House, Publishers. DAISY; FORGET-ME-NOT; ROSE; VIOLET from *Secrets of Flowers* as revealed by A. Stoddard Kull. Copyright © 1976, 1966 by The Stephen Greene Press. FEBRUARY GREETINGS by Adeline Roseberg. Previously published in *The Farmer,* January 1976. THE LITTLE GIRL NEXT DOOR by Helen Wing, from *Child Life* Magazine. Copyright 1926, 1954 by Rand McNally & Company.

Statement of ownership, management and circulation (Required by 39 U.S.C., 3685), of IDEALS, published 8 times a year in: Jan., Feb., Apr., June, July, Sept., Oct., Nov., at Milwaukee, Wisconsin for September 1979. Publisher, Ideals Publishing Corporation; Editorial Director, James A. Kuse; Managing Editor, Ralph Luedtke; Owner, Harlequin Holding, Inc., 306 South State Street, Dover, Delaware 19901. The known bondholders, mortgagees, and other security holders owning or holding 1 percent or more of total amount of bonds, mortgages or other securities are: None. Average no. copies each issue during preceding 12 months: Total no. copies printed (Net Press Run) 296,558. Paid circulation 93,483. Mail subscriptions 142,605. Total paid circulation 236,088. Free distribution 638. Total distribution 236,726. Single issue published nearest to filing date: Total no. copies printed (Net Press Run) 628,780. Paid circulation 280,330. Other sales 52,392. Free distribution 359. Total distribution 333,081. I certify that the statements made by me above are correct and complete. William G. Gaspero, President/C.E.O.

COLOR ART AND PHOTO CREDITS
(in order of appearance)

Front and back cover, Ralph Luedtke; inside front cover, Gerald Koser; Valentine message, Colour Library International (USA) Limited; A gift of roses, Gerald Koser; Red roses, Colour Library International (USA) Limited; Cherry pie, Gerald Koser; Valentine's Day party, Gerald Koser; Love's melody, Colour Library International (USA) Limited; Valentine gifts, Gerald Koser; LOVE LETTERS, Jean Honoré Fragonard, The Frick Collection, New York; Roses and lace, Colour Library International (USA) Limited; Old-fashioned valentine with pansies, Kean Archive, photo by Gerald Koser; Valentine postcard, Sourpuss, Civil War and Radio Bug Valentines, Kean Archives, photo by Gerald Koser; Ornamental Valentine and valentine postcards, Kean Archives, and "I never loved until . . . " postcard, Geraldine Zisk, photo by Gerald Koser; Ornamental and fancy valentines, Kean Archives, photo by Gerald Koser; School days valentines, Gerald Koser; Rag dolls, Gerald Koser; Family by the fire, Four By Five, Inc.; Winter Woods, Art Riley; Skiers at Mount Bachelor near Bend, Oregon, Freelance Photographers Guild; Moraine Lake, Banff National Park, Alberta, Canada, Colour Library International (USA) Limited; Grand Canyon National Park, Arizona, Josef Muench; Cardinal, A. Devaney, Inc.; inside back cover, Colour Library International (USA) Limited.

The FIRST Ideals
COLLECTOR'S PLATE

1980 Mother's Day Plate
by Frances Hook

created by
Woodmere China

Actual Size 8½"

A precious time
preserved forever . . .
limited edition . . .
superbly crafted porcelain

SPECIAL NOTICE

Due to the limited quantity available, we are offering this exquisite Collector's Plate to regular IDEALS readers first. Only one out of every hundred readers will be able to receive this special edition plate. Order early! Orders will be processed on a first-come, first-served basis.

Anna Reese Jarvis died May 9, 1905, without realizing her dream of establishing a national holiday that would honor mothers. Her daughter, Philadelphia schoolteacher Anna M. Jarvis, was unmarried and lived alone with her blind sister. Anna M. Jarvis felt the loss of her mother so deeply that she was determined to establish a special day in honor of all mothers. On May 9, 1914, President Woodrow Wilson proclaimed the second Sunday in May "Mother's Day," and formally recognized Miss Anna Jarvis as its founder.

Now you can share in the warmth of this occasion with the First Edition of an Ideals Collector's Plate—the 1980 Mother's Day Plate.

Specially created for Ideals by Woodmere China, one of America's most renowned producers of fine art porcelain china, this finely crafted work of art is 8½ inches in diameter and handsomely bordered with 24 karat gold.

The plate features an original work of art from the Ideals Collection first published in **Neighborly IDEALS** 1966.

The 1980 Mother's Day Plate is strictly limited to an edition of 5,000. Each plate is hand-numbered on the reverse side and arrives with a Certificate of Authenticity to firmly establish its value.

This is your opportunity to become among the first to own a Collector's Plate by Ideals. It is a wonderful way to start a new collection, a striking edition to an existing collection, or a unique gift for that special Mother—yours!

As Ideals' first work in porcelain china, this Collector's Plate is destined to have permanent, enduring worth. Anyone who may wish to acquire this plate in the future will have to obtain it from an original subscriber.

Order today! This sequentially-numbered edition will be a remembrance to treasure now . . . and in the years that follow.

Fill in the Reservation Certificate on the reverse side of this form, enclose your check, money-order or credit card information, and seal in this self-enclosing form.

Ideals 1980 Mother's Day Plate Reservation Certificate

Please reserve_____personal edition(s) of the 1980 Mother's Day Plate, bearing the original work of art by Frances Hook at the original issue price of $29.95, plus $1.50 postage and handling. I have enclosed a total of $31.45* (payment in full) as indicated: 27962

□ CHECK   □ MONEY ORDER   PLEASE CHARGE MY   □   MASTER CHARGE
BP01   Remit In U.S. Funds   □   BANKAMERICARD/VISA

NAME _____   Signature_____

ADDRESS_____   Account No. ⬚⬚⬚⬚⬚⬚⬚⬚⬚⬚⬚⬚⬚⬚⬚⬚⬚

CITY _____

STATE _____ZIP _____   Expires ⬚⬚⬚⬚

*Wisconsin Residents Add 4% ($1.20) Sales Tax   All Orders Subject To Approval

FOLD HERE FIRST

FOLD SIDE FLAPS FIRST — THEN FOLD HERE

When properly sealed with the above gummed flap this envelope and its contents will travel safely through the mail.

THANK YOU!

from

ZIP CODE

ideals
PUBLISHING CORPORATION
175 COMMUNITY DRIVE
GREAT NECK, NEW YORK 11025

FOLD HERE FIRST

ABOUT THE PLATE: "MOTHERS OVER THE FENCE"

The painting featured on the 1980 Ideals Mother's Day Plate originally appeared in a 1966 issue of *Ideals* magazine. The editors of Ideals, in concert with the artist, utilized their talents to produce a visual representation of the warmth and friendliness exhibited by mothers and children everywhere.

The painting was originally done in 1965, a period during which this country experienced a great deal of political and social unrest. With that in mind,

models were posed in a setting and dressed in a mode which depicted an earlier and somewhat more tranquil place and time.

The end result was and is an exquisite painting depicting the warmth of neighboring mothers and their children while blending the delights of real life within a framework of delicate fantasy.

Appropriately, this 1980 Mother's Day Plate acknowledges the many mothers who embody warmth, love, and neighborliness.